DID YOU KNOW? A FUN-FILLED FAMILY FACT BOOK

AMANDA ALIFF, LPC

TABLE OF CONTENTS

Chapter 9:
Conclusion: Keep Learning, Keep Laughing

CHAPTER 1

INTRODUCTION: THE JOY OF LEARNING TOGETHER

How to Use This Book

Welcome to 'Did You Know? A Fun-Filled Family Fact Book!' – your ticket to a world of fascinating facts and hilarious tidbits. This book is designed to be a family adventure, so gather 'round and get ready for some mind-blowing discoveries! Whether you're a curious kid or a knowledge-hungry grown-up, there's something here for everyone. So, how do you use this book? Well, it's as easy as opening to any page and letting the fun begin!

Each page is packed with incredible facts that will make you say 'Wow!' and 'No way!' But don't just read silently to yourself – share these nuggets of wisdom out loud! Take turns being the 'Fact Master' and watch as jaws drop and giggles erupt. And here's a pro tip: keep this book handy during family dinners, long car rides, or any time you need a quick dose of amazement. It's the perfect conversation starter and boredom buster all rolled into one!

Remember, there's no right or wrong way to enjoy this book. Flip through the pages randomly, or start from the beginning and work your way through. Challenge each other to remember the craziest facts, or use them as inspiration for your own research adventures. The most important rule? Have fun! So, are you ready to dive into a world of wonder? Let's get started and see just how many 'Did you know?' moments we can share together!

The Benefits of Family Learning

Did you know that learning together as a family can be a barrel of laughs and a boatload of fun? It's true! When parents and kids dive into new facts and ideas side by side, something magical happens. Not only do you all get smarter (yes, even you, Mom and Dad!), but you also create hilarious inside jokes and memories that'll last longer than that 'unbreakable' toy your kid got last Christmas.

But wait, there's more! Family learning isn't just about filling your brains with fascinating facts. It's like a secret sauce for bonding, helping you grow closer faster than a weed in your backyard. When you explore the weird and wonderful world of knowledge together, you're not just learning about the universe - you're learning about each other too. Plus, it gives kids a chance to see their parents scratching their heads and saying, 'Huh, I never knew that!' Talk about a confidence booster!

So, buckle up, family! This book is your ticket to a wild ride through the land of 'Did You Know?' Get ready to giggle, gasp, and gawk at mind-blowing facts that'll make your family gatherings more entertaining than a monkey on a unicycle. Who knows? By the time you're done, you might just be the smartest, silliest family on the block. And isn't that what every family aspires to be?

Tips for Engaging Discussions

Engaging in discussions about the fun facts you've learned is half the joy of this book! To get the most out of your family reading time, try asking open-ended questions like, 'What do you think about that?' or 'How do you think this fact relates to our daily lives?' These questions encourage critical thinking and help children connect new information to their existing knowledge.

Another great tip is to turn fact-sharing into a game. Challenge family members to remember facts from previous reading sessions, or have a contest to see who can come up with the most creative way to apply a new piece of information. This not only makes learning more enjoyable but also helps reinforce the facts in everyone's memory.

Lastly, don't be afraid to let conversations wander off-topic. Sometimes, the most interesting discussions start with a fun fact but end up exploring entirely new territories of curiosity. Embrace these moments as opportunities for further learning and bonding. Remember, the goal is not just to memorize facts, but to foster a love for learning and discovery that will last a lifetime!

CHAPTER 2

WACKY WORLD OF SCIENCE

Mind-Blowing Biology Facts

Did you know that your body is home to trillions of tiny organisms? That's right, folks! Your skin, gut, and even your belly button are like bustling cities for bacteria, fungi, and other microbes. But don't worry, most of these little critters are actually helping you out. They're like your personal army of microscopic housekeepers, keeping things clean and balanced. So the next time you hear someone say 'eww, germs!', you can tell them that not all microbes are bad guys!

Ever wondered why your cat's eyes glow in the dark? It's not because they're secretly aliens (although that would be pretty cool). Cats, along with many other nocturnal animals, have a special layer in their eyes called the tapetum lucidum. This layer acts like a built-in night vision goggle, reflecting light back through the retina and giving them super-powered night vision. So when you see those glowing eyes in the dark, just remember: your furry friend isn't plotting world domination, they're just really good at seeing in the dark!

Here's a mind-bender for you: did you know that you're not entirely human? Don't panic, we're not talking about secret alien DNA. It turns out that only about 43% of the cells in your body are human cells. The rest? They're microbes! That's right, you're basically walking around in a microbe suit. But before you start feeling like a stranger in your own skin, remember that these little lodgers are essential for your health. They help digest your food, boost your immune system, and even influence your mood. So next time you look in the mirror, give a little wave to your microscopic roommates!

Crazy Chemistry Tidbits

Did you know that chemistry can be absolutely bonkers? Get ready for some mind-blowing facts that'll make your head spin faster than a centrifuge! For instance, did you know that there's a metal so reactive it explodes when it touches water? It's called francium, and it's so rare that only a few grams exist on Earth at any given time. Talk about a splashy entrance!

But wait, there's more! Ever heard of 'heavy water'? No, it's not what happens when you forget to take the ice cubes out of your drink. It's actually water where the hydrogen atoms have been replaced with deuterium, a heavier version of hydrogen. And get this - if you drank nothing but heavy water, you'd eventually get sick because your body's chemical reactions would slow down. So much for that 'heavy water diet' idea!

Last but not least, let's talk about the world's smelliest substance. It's called thioacetone, and it's so stinky that a single drop can make an entire town smell like rotten eggs! In fact, in 1889, some German scientists accidentally unleashed its odor, causing people to flee the area and triggering cases of vomiting and fainting. Now that's what we call a real stink bomb! Remember, kids: chemistry is cool, but maybe leave the super-smelly stuff to the professionals!

Physics Phenomena That Will Surprise You

Did you know that light can bend? It's true! When light travels from one medium to another, like from air to water, it changes direction. This is why a straw in a glass of water looks bent, or why your legs appear shorter when you're standing in a swimming pool. It's not magic, it's just physics playing tricks on our eyes!

Have you ever wondered why you can't walk through walls like a superhero? It's all thanks to a quirky quantum physics concept called the Pauli Exclusion Principle. This principle states that no two electrons can occupy the same quantum state at the same time. In simpler terms, it's like trying to fit two people into the same seat at a movie theater - it just doesn't work! This principle is what gives matter its 'solidness' and prevents us from walking through walls. Sorry, superheroes!

Gravity isn't just about keeping your feet on the ground - it can also make time slow down! According to Einstein's theory of relativity, time moves slower in stronger gravitational fields. This means that time actually passes slightly faster at the top of a skyscraper than at ground level. Don't worry though, the difference is too small for us to notice in everyday life. But next time you're running late, you can always blame it on gravity!

Earth and Space Oddities

Did you know that our planet Earth is not a perfect sphere? It's actually shaped like a squished ball, slightly flattened at the poles and bulging at the equator. Scientists call this shape an 'oblate spheroid,' but we like to think of it as Earth's way of letting out its belt after a big meal of asteroids and space dust!

Speaking of space oddities, have you ever wondered why Saturn gets all the attention with its flashy rings? Well, it turns out that all the gas giants in our solar system - Jupiter, Saturn, Uranus, and Neptune - have rings! Saturn just happens to be the show-off of the bunch, with rings so big and bright that even Galileo could see them with his telescope back in 1610. The other planets are probably just jealous of Saturn's bling!

And here's a mind-bending fact that might make you feel a bit dizzy: did you know that the Earth is spinning faster now than it was a century ago? That's right, our planet is picking up speed like a cosmic merry-go-round! Scientists think it might be due to melting glaciers or movements in the Earth's core. So the next time you feel like there aren't enough hours in the day, you can blame it on our planet's need for speed!

CHAPTER 3

HILARIOUS HISTORY

Bizarre Customs from the Past

Hold onto your hats, folks, because we're about to dive into some of the wackiest customs from the past! Did you know that in medieval England, people believed that carrying a potato in their pocket would cure rheumatism? That's right, instead of seeing a doctor, they'd just stuff a spud in their trousers and hope for the best. Can you imagine walking around with your pockets full of mashed potatoes? Talk about a lumpy fashion statement!

But wait, there's more! In ancient Rome, people thought it was good luck to sneeze, so they would actually try to make themselves sneeze on purpose. They'd tickle their noses with feathers or sniff strong spices to get a good 'a-choo' going. Next time you sneeze and someone says 'bless you,' you can tell them you're just following an ancient Roman tradition of bringing good fortune. Just maybe don't mention the part about the feather tickling!

And here's a real head-scratcher: in 16th century Europe, it was fashionable for men to wear codpieces - that's a pouch attached to the front of their trousers to, ahem, enhance certain areas. These weren't just any pouches, though. They were often brightly colored, heavily padded, and decorated with jewels or ribbons. Imagine walking down the street and seeing a bunch of guys with bejeweled pillows strapped to their pants! It gives a whole new meaning to the phrase 'fashion statement,' doesn't it?

Funny Failures That Changed the World

Did you know that some of the world's greatest inventions were actually happy accidents? It's true! Take the microwave oven, for example. In 1945, engineer Percy Spencer was working on radar technology when he noticed the chocolate bar in his pocket had melted. Oops! But instead of just changing his pants, he decided to investigate. His tasty mistake led to the creation of the microwave oven, forever changing how we heat up our leftovers and pop our popcorn!

Another funny failure that changed the world happened in 1853 when chef George Crum accidentally created potato chips. A picky customer kept sending back his fried potatoes, complaining they were too thick and soggy. Frustrated, Crum sliced the potatoes paper-thin, fried them to a crisp, and drowned them in salt. To his surprise, the customer loved them! And just like that, the potato chip was born, giving us the perfect crunchy snack to munch on while we watch our favorite shows.

Even the beloved Popsicle was a delicious mistake! In 1905, 11-year-old Frank Epperson left a cup of powdered soda and water outside overnight with the stirring stick still in it. The next morning, he found a frozen treat on a stick! He called it the 'Epsicle,' but later changed the name to 'Popsicle.' So, the next time you enjoy a cool, refreshing Popsicle on a hot summer day, remember to thank young Frank and his forgetfulness!

Peculiar People in History

Did you know that history is full of people who were, well, a bit odd? Take Emperor Norton I, for example. In 1859, Joshua Norton of San Francisco declared himself 'Emperor of the United States' and 'Protector of Mexico.' The funny thing is, people went along with it! He printed his own money, which local shops accepted, and even had his own imperial uniform. Talk about taking 'dress-up' to a whole new level!

Then there's Tarrare, a French showman with an appetite that would make competitive eaters look like picky toddlers. This guy could eat anything - and we mean anything! He once swallowed a whole eel without chewing and could eat a meal intended for 15 people in one sitting. Doctors were so baffled by his endless hunger that they used him as a military courier, hiding messages in boxes that he would swallow and, um, 'deliver' later. Now that's what we call a 'special delivery'!

Let's not forget about Timothy Dexter, the self-proclaimed 'Lord of the Universe.' This eccentric American businessman made a fortune by accidentally making smart business decisions. He once shipped warming pans (used for warming beds) to the West Indies, a tropical region. Instead of being a disaster, the locals used them as ladles for molasses and Dexter made a huge profit! He even faked his own death to see who would attend his funeral. Now that's taking 'fashionably late' to a whole new level!

Wacky Wars and Silly Skirmishes

Did you know that some wars were fought over the silliest things? Take the War of the Oaken Bucket, for example. In 1325, soldiers from Bologna and Modena in Italy actually fought over a stolen wooden bucket! Can you imagine risking your life for a bucket? It's like having a food fight, but with swords and shields instead of mashed potatoes!

And let's not forget about the Emu War of 1932 in Australia. The Australian military declared war on... emus! Yes, those big, flightless birds that look like they're wearing feathery tuxedos. The emus were destroying crops, so soldiers were sent to stop them. But guess what? The emus won! They outran and outsmarted the soldiers, proving that sometimes bird brains are better than human ones!

Even cats have started wars! In 1969, Honduras and El Salvador fought a war that was partly triggered by a soccer match. But did you know it was nicknamed the 'Football War' or the 'Soccer War'? It's like the ultimate sports rivalry gone wrong! Next time you're watching a game and things get heated, just remember: at least you're not starting an international conflict over it!

CHAPTER 4

GEOGRAPHY GIGGLES

Weird Places Around the World

Did you know that our world is full of wacky and wonderful places that seem too strange to be real? Get ready to giggle and gasp as we explore some of the weirdest locations on Earth! From a town where chickens outnumber people to a forest where the trees grow upside down, these places will make you wonder if you've stepped into a real-life cartoon.

Imagine visiting a village where everyone lives in houses shaped like mushrooms, or a beach with sand that squeaks when you walk on it! These aren't make-believe places from a storybook – they actually exist! Pack your bags (and your sense of humor) as we embark on a hilarious journey to discover the most bizarre and belly-laugh-inducing spots around the globe.

But wait, there's more! Have you ever heard of a lake that's pink, a island filled with rabbits, or a hotel made entirely of salt? These quirky destinations prove that sometimes, truth is stranger (and funnier) than fiction. So, gather your family, put on your explorer hats, and get ready to learn about places so weird, you'll have to see them to believe them!

Amusing Animal Habitats

Did you know that some animals have the most hilarious and unexpected living arrangements? Take the burrowing owl, for example. These pint-sized comedians of the bird world have a knack for home invasion – they often move into abandoned prairie dog holes! Imagine the surprise on a prairie dog's face when it returns home to find a feathered squatter in its living room. It's like nature's version of a sitcom roommate situation!

But wait, there's more! Have you heard about the clownfish and its peculiar choice of roommate? These little orange jokesters make their homes in the tentacles of sea anemones. That's right, they willingly snuggle up to a creature that stings most other fish! It's as if they're saying, 'Who needs a soft, comfy bed when you can have a prickly, venomous one instead?' Talk about an extreme home makeover!

And let's not forget about the hermit crab, the ultimate real estate flipper of the animal kingdom. These crafty crustaceans are always on the lookout for bigger and better shells to call home. When they outgrow their current abode, they simply pop into a new one, like trying on clothes at a thrift store. Sometimes, they even form 'conga lines' where they swap shells in order of size. It's like a bizarre game of musical chairs, but with portable homes!

Laughable Landmarks

Did you know that some landmarks around the world are so silly, they'll make you giggle? Take the Big Banana in Australia, for example. It's exactly what it sounds like – a giant banana-shaped building that's longer than a school bus! Imagine trying to peel that for your lunchbox. You'd need a ladder and some really strong arms!

But wait, there's more! In Belgium, you can visit a building shaped like a giant atom. It's called the Atomium, and it looks like a massive science experiment gone wild. The best part? You can actually go inside and pretend you're a tiny electron zooming around. Just don't get too dizzy from all that orbiting!

And let's not forget about the Crooked House in Poland. This wacky building looks like it's melting in the sun, with wavy walls and wonky windows. It's so crooked, you might think you need glasses just to look at it straight! But don't worry, it's not going to fall over – it's just designed to make you laugh and scratch your head at the same time.

Curious Cultures and Traditions

Did you know that in Japan, it's considered polite to slurp your noodles? That's right, kids! While your parents might tell you off for making noise at the dinner table, in Japan, the louder you slurp, the more you're complimenting the chef. So next time you're eating spaghetti, just tell your folks you're practicing Japanese etiquette!

Ever heard of the La Tomatina festival in Spain? It's like a food fight, but way messier! Once a year, thousands of people gather in the town of Buñol to throw squished tomatoes at each other. Imagine coming home covered head to toe in tomato sauce - you'd look like a walking pizza! Just remember, if you ever visit Spain during this festival, don't wear your favorite white t-shirt!

In Thailand, they celebrate the New Year with a giant water fight called Songkran. For three whole days, people roam the streets with water guns, buckets, and hoses, soaking anyone they see. It's like a country-wide game of water tag! So if you're planning a family trip to Thailand in April, don't forget to pack your swimsuit and get ready for the wettest, wildest New Year's party you've ever seen!

CHAPTER 5

THE HUMAN BODY'S HIDDEN SECRETS

Surprising Facts About Your Brain

Did you know that your brain is like a super-computer that never stops working? Even when you're fast asleep, your brain is busy sorting through memories, solving problems, and coming up with wild ideas for your next adventure! It's no wonder you sometimes wake up with a brilliant solution to yesterday's homework puzzle or a crazy dream about flying pizzas!

Here's another mind-boggling fact: your brain uses about 20% of all the energy your body produces, even though it only makes up about 2% of your body weight. That's right, your brain is an energy-guzzling machine! So the next time your parents tell you to eat your vegetables, remember that you're not just feeding your tummy, you're fueling your brain's incredible power!

And get this: your brain has about 86 billion neurons, which are like tiny messengers that help different parts of your brain talk to each other. If you tried to count all those neurons, it would take you over 2,700 years! That's longer than the time between the ancient Egyptians building the pyramids and you reading this book right now. Pretty amazing, huh?

Digestive System Silliness

Did you know that your digestive system is like a wacky amusement park for your food? Imagine your mouth as the ticket booth, where food gets its first thrilling ride on the Tongue Coaster! Then, it zooms down the Esophagus

Slide, making a splash into the Stomach Whirlpool. Hold on tight, because things are about to get really silly!

Next up, your food takes a wild journey through the Intestine Maze. It's like a crazy water park slide that's over 20 feet long! As your food zooms through, it meets friendly bacteria that help break it down. These tiny helpers are like the world's tiniest chefs, cooking up nutrients for your body to use. By the time your food reaches the end of this wacky ride, it's completely transformed!

But wait, there's more! Did you know that your body can make some pretty funny noises during digestion? Those growls and gurgles you hear are actually your gut's way of saying 'Woohoo! What a ride!' So next time your tummy rumbles, just remember it's throwing its own little party in there. Isn't the human body amazing and hilarious?

The Marvels of Human Senses

Did you know that your nose can detect over a trillion different scents? That's right, your schnoz is like a super-powered smell detector! While we often take our sense of smell for granted, it's actually quite remarkable. Just imagine all the delicious (and sometimes not-so-delicious) odors you encounter every day – from freshly baked cookies to your brother's stinky socks!

But wait, there's more! Your taste buds aren't just hanging out on your tongue for fun. These tiny flavor detectives can distinguish between sweet, salty, sour, bitter, and umami tastes. And here's a fun fact that might make you say 'Eww!': your taste buds are constantly being replaced. Every two weeks, you get a brand new set! So the next time your parents serve up some Brussels sprouts, just remember – in two weeks, you'll have fresh taste buds to try them with!

Now, let's not forget about our eyes – they're not just for giving your siblings the stink eye! Your peepers are actually incredibly complex organs that can distinguish between millions of different colors. And get this: your eyes never grow bigger after you're born. That's right, you're born with your adult-sized eyeballs! So the next time someone tells you that you have your mother's eyes, you can say, 'Yep, and they've been this size since day one!'

Skeletal and Muscular Mysteries

Did you know that your skeleton is not just a bunch of boring old bones? It's actually a living, growing part of your body that's full of surprises! For instance, did you know that babies are born with about 300 bones, but adults only have 206? That's right, as we grow up, some of our bones fuse together like puzzle pieces. It's nature's way of saying, 'Let's make you a little less rattly!'

Now, let's flex those brain muscles and learn about our actual muscles! Did you know that you use about 300 muscles just to keep your balance when you're standing still? That's like having a whole team of tiny acrobats working together inside your body! And here's a giggle-worthy fact: the strongest muscle in your body, relative to its size, is in your jaw. So the next time your parents tell you to stop talking, you can say you're just exercising the most powerful muscle you have!

CHAPTER 6

TECHNOLOGY AND INVENTIONS: FROM SILLY TO SERIOUS

Accidental Inventions That Changed Everything

Did you know that some of the world's most useful inventions were actually created by accident? It's true! Sometimes, the best ideas come when we're not even looking for them. Imagine spilling your drink and discovering a new type of fabric, or forgetting about a experiment and finding a life-saving medicine. That's exactly how some of our favorite inventions came to be!

Take the microwave oven, for example. It was invented when a scientist named Percy Spencer was working with radar equipment and noticed that the chocolate bar in his pocket had melted. Oops! But instead of just getting upset about his gooey pants, he wondered why it happened. His curiosity led to the creation of the microwave oven, which now helps families heat up leftovers and make popcorn for movie nights in record time!

Another silly accident turned serious invention is the Post-it Note. A scientist was trying to create a super strong adhesive but ended up with a super weak one instead. Bummer, right? Wrong! His colleague realized this not-so-sticky glue was perfect for bookmarks that wouldn't damage pages. Now, thanks to this happy mistake, we can stick reminders all over the house without leaving marks. So next time you make a mistake, remember: it might just be the next big invention waiting to happen!

Gadgets That Never Caught On

Did you know that some inventions were so wacky, they never made it to your local gadget store? Imagine trying to type on a keyboard made entirely of bubble wrap – pop, pop, pop with every letter! Or picture yourself wearing a hat with a built-in umbrella that opens automatically when it rains. These silly gadgets might sound fun, but they're just a few examples of the many inventions that never quite caught on with the public.

One particularly amusing gadget that failed to impress was the 'Smell-O-Vision,' a device designed to release scents during movies. Can you imagine watching a cooking show and suddenly smelling freshly baked cookies? While it might sound delicious, moviegoers weren't too keen on having their noses bombarded with various odors throughout a film. Another quirky invention was the 'Banana Slicer,' a plastic contraption meant to perfectly slice bananas. But as it turns out, most people were pretty happy using a regular old knife!

These funny flops remind us that not every invention becomes the next smartphone or microwave oven. Sometimes, the silliest ideas can teach us valuable lessons about what people really need and want. So the next time you have a wild idea for a new gadget, remember these goofy gizmos and ask yourself: Will people actually use this, or will it end up in the 'Gadgets That Never Caught On' hall of fame?

Future Tech That Sounds Like Science Fiction

Hold onto your hoverboards, folks! The future is zooming towards us faster than a speeding rocket, and it's bringing some seriously cool gadgets along for the ride. Remember those sci-fi movies where people could control computers with their minds? Well, guess what? Scientists are already working on brain-computer interfaces that could make that a reality! Imagine changing the TV channel just by thinking about it - no more fighting over the remote!

But wait, there's more! How about clothes that can change color or pattern with the tap of an app? Or windows that turn into TV screens? These aren't just wild dreams anymore; they're technologies in development right now. And for all you foodie families out there, get ready for 3D-printed meals! Yep, you read that right - your dinner could come out of a printer someday. Talk about fast food!

Now, here's a mind-bender for you: quantum computers. These super-smart machines could solve problems in seconds that would take our current computers thousands of years! They might even help us talk to aliens (if they're out there). So, the next time someone tells you that your ideas are too 'out there,' just remember: in the world of future tech, nothing's too silly to be serious!

Everyday Items with Unexpected Origins

Did you know that some of the everyday items we use have surprisingly quirky origins? Take the humble tea bag, for instance. This convenient little packet wasn't invented by a tea company at all – it was accidentally created by a tea importer named Thomas Sullivan in 1908. He sent samples of tea to his customers in small silk bags, intending them to remove the tea before brewing. But his clever customers dunked the whole bag in hot water, and voila! The tea bag was born!

Speaking of accidental inventions, let's talk about one of the stickiest situations in history – the creation of Super Glue! In 1942, Dr. Harry Coover was actually trying to make clear plastic gun sights for soldiers. Instead, he ended up with a substance that stuck to everything it touched. Talk about a happy mistake! It wasn't until years later that someone realized this super sticky stuff could be incredibly useful. Now, thanks to Dr. Coover's 'oops' moment, we can fix just about anything – except maybe our parents' rule about no jumping on the bed!

And here's a fact that might make you go 'Ew!' – did you know that the original Coca-Cola contained cocaine? Yes, you read that right! When it was first invented in 1886 by pharmacist John Pemberton, Coca-Cola was marketed as a cure for various ailments and contained a small amount of cocaine from coca leaves. Don't worry, though – the cocaine was removed from the recipe in 1903. So the next time you enjoy a cold Coke, remember: it used to be a very different kind of pick-me-up!

CHAPTER 7

NATURE'S NUTTY SIDE

Plants with Peculiar Properties

Did you know that some plants have superpowers? Well, not exactly like Superman, but they do have some pretty peculiar properties that might make you say 'Wow!' Take the sensitive plant, for example. This shy little guy is so jumpy that it actually folds up its leaves and droops when you touch it! It's like the plant version of playing dead, except it's just trying to avoid being eaten by animals. Talk about a drama queen of the plant world!

But wait, there's more! Have you ever heard of a plant that can eat animals? Meet the Venus flytrap, nature's very own bug zapper! This carnivorous plant has leaves that snap shut faster than you can say 'gotcha!' when an unsuspecting insect lands on it. It's like a tiny, green version of those claw machines at the arcade, except this one always wins its prize. Just don't stick your finger in there, or you might end up as plant food!

And let's not forget about the stinky stars of the plant world. The corpse flower and the skunk cabbage are two plants that smell so bad, they could clear a room faster than your dad's cheesiest joke! These smelly celebrities use their awful odor to attract pollinators who think they've found a delicious rotting meal. It's like nature's version of a stink bomb, but with a purpose. Who knew plants could be so grossly fascinating?

Animal Kingdom Comedians

Did you know that the animal kingdom is full of natural comedians? Take the penguin, for example. These tuxedo-clad birds waddle around like tiny butlers, slipping and sliding on the ice in a slapstick routine that would make Charlie Chaplin proud. And let's not forget their impressive 'belly slides' - it's as if they're auditioning for the world's most adorable luge team!

But penguins aren't the only jokesters in the animal world. Have you ever seen a proboscis monkey? With their big, floppy noses and potbellies, they look like they've stepped right out of a cartoon. These monkeys spend their days swinging through the trees, making funny faces, and honking loudly - it's like they're hosting their own comedy show in the jungles of Borneo!

Even underwater, the laughs keep coming. The pufferfish, when threatened, inflates itself to look like a spiky beach ball. It's nature's version of 'puff out your cheeks and hold your breath' - only much more impressive (and a lot safer for the pufferfish). So next time you're feeling down, just remember: somewhere out there, a penguin is probably faceplanting into the snow, a monkey is making a goofy face, and a fish is turning itself into a living balloon. Nature truly has a nutty side!

Wacky Weather Phenomena

Did you know that sometimes it rains animals? It's true! In some parts of the world, people have reported frogs, fish, and even small crabs falling from the sky. But don't worry, these creatures aren't magically appearing out of thin air. Scientists believe that strong winds or waterspouts can pick up small animals from bodies of water and carry them for miles before dropping them back down to Earth. Imagine the surprise on your family's faces when you tell them about the day it rained cats and dogs... well, frogs and fish!

Have you ever heard of a fire rainbow? Despite its name, it's not actually a rainbow and has nothing to do with fire! This rare and beautiful weather phenomenon is officially called a circumhorizontal arc. It occurs when sunlight refracts through ice crystals in high-altitude cirrus clouds, creating a colorful, horizontal streak across the sky. The next time you're cloud-watching with your family, keep an eye out for this magical display. Just remember, if you spot one, it's not a sign that the sky is on fire – it's just Mother Nature showing off her artistic side!

Let's talk about something that sounds like it came straight out of a superhero movie: ball lightning. This mysterious phenomenon appears as glowing, electric orbs floating through the air during thunderstorms. While scientists are still scratching their heads about exactly how it forms, eyewitnesses have reported seeing these eerie spheres pass through walls and windows! So, the next time there's a thunderstorm, gather the family together and see if you can spot one of these natural light shows. Just remember to stay safe indoors – we don't want anyone getting zapped while trying to become the next Thor!

Ecosystem Eccentricities

Did you know that nature has a quirky sense of humor? Take the sloth, for example. These slow-moving creatures have such a sluggish metabolism that they only need to go to the bathroom once a week! And when they do, it's quite an event. Sloths will climb down from their treetop homes, dig a hole, do their business, and then cover it up - all while doing a little 'poo-dance' that scientists are still trying to figure out. Talk about a wacky weekly ritual!

But sloths aren't the only oddballs in the ecosystem. Have you ever heard of the pistol shrimp? This tiny crustacean packs a punch that would make any superhero jealous. It has one oversized claw that it can snap shut so fast, it creates a bubble that collapses with a loud 'pop' and a flash of light. This sonic boom is so powerful it can stun or even kill small fish. Imagine if your snaps could do that - you'd be the hit of every talent show!

And let's not forget about the leafcutter ants, nature's tiny farmers. These industrious insects don't actually eat the leaves they cut - instead, they use them to grow fungus gardens underground. That's right, they're fungus farmers! They cultivate their crops with such care that they even use antibiotics to keep their fungus healthy. So the next time you see a line of ants carrying leaves, just remember - they're not on a picnic, they're heading to work on their mushroom farm!

CHAPTER 8

FOOD FOR THOUGHT (AND LAUGHTER)

Strange Eating Habits Around the World

Did you know that in some parts of the world, people eat things that might make your tummy do a little dance? Let's take a tasty tour around the globe and discover some of the wackiest eating habits! From crunchy critters to stinky delicacies, we're about to embark on a flavor adventure that'll make your taste buds giggle and your nose wrinkle in surprise.

In Japan, some brave eaters munch on live octopus tentacles that still wriggle on the plate! Can you imagine trying to eat your dinner while it's trying to escape? Meanwhile, in Iceland, folks enjoy a treat called hákarl, which is fermented shark meat that smells like stinky socks. Yum... or yuck? And let's not forget about the Philippines, where balut - a partially developed duck egg - is considered a delicious snack. It's like a surprise egg, but the surprise might make you say 'Eek!' instead of 'Yay!'

But wait, there's more! In China, bird's nest soup is a luxury dish made from the saliva of swiftlets. That's right, bird spit soup! And in Scotland, haggis - a mixture of sheep organs, oatmeal, and spices cooked inside a sheep's stomach - is a beloved national dish. So, the next time you turn up your nose at broccoli, remember that somewhere in the world, someone is happily munching on bugs or slurping down a bowl of bird spit soup. Suddenly, those green trees on your plate don't seem so bad, do they?

Food Facts That Will Blow Your Mind

Did you know that some of the most common foods we eat every day have mind-blowing secrets? Let's dive into the world of food facts that will make your jaw drop and your taste buds tingle with excitement! From the origins of your favorite snacks to the hidden powers of everyday ingredients, we're about to embark on a delicious adventure that will change the way you look at your plate forever.

First up, let's talk about everyone's favorite fruit impersonator - the tomato! That's right, this saucy superstar is actually a fruit, not a vegetable. But wait, there's more! In 1893, the U.S. Supreme Court legally declared tomatoes to be vegetables. Talk about a real identity crisis! And here's a corny fact for you: did you know that an average ear of corn has an even number of rows, usually 16? Mother Nature sure loves her symmetry!

Now, let's spice things up with some hot facts about everyone's favorite condiment - ketchup! In the 1830s, ketchup was sold as medicine. Imagine trying to cure a headache with a squirt of ketchup on your forehead! And if you're a fan of spicy food, here's a cool fact to balance out the heat: spicy foods don't actually burn your taste buds. The sensation is all in your brain! So next time your little brother says his tongue is on fire after eating a jalapeño, you can tell him it's all in his head - literally!

Culinary Disasters That Became Delicacies

Did you know that some of our favorite foods were actually born out of kitchen blunders? It's true! Imagine a world without chocolate chip cookies or potato chips. Well, buckle up, food fans, because we're about to take a tasty trip through the land of 'Oops, I made something delicious!' These culinary catastrophes turned into mouthwatering miracles will have you looking at your kitchen disasters in a whole new light.

Take the beloved chocolate chip cookie, for instance. In 1930, Ruth Wakefield was baking her usual batch of butter drop cookies when she realized she was out of baker's chocolate. In a moment of desperation (or genius), she chopped up a Nestle's semi-sweet chocolate bar and tossed it into the dough, expecting it to melt. But surprise, surprise! The chips held their shape, and voila - the chocolate chip cookie was born. Talk about a sweet mistake!

And let's not forget about the crispy, crunchy potato chip. Legend has it that in 1853, a chef named George Crum was having a bad day when a picky customer kept sending back his fried potatoes, complaining they were too thick. In a fit of frustration, Crum sliced the potatoes paper-thin, fried them to a crisp, and drowned them in salt. To his shock, the customer loved them! So next time you're munching on these snacks, remember: sometimes the best recipes come from a pinch of accident and a dash of 'Oh no!'

The Science Behind Taste and Flavor

Did you know that your taste buds are like tiny flavor detectives? These microscopic marvels work tirelessly to help you distinguish between sweet, salty, sour, bitter, and umami flavors. But here's the kicker: your nose is the real MVP of the taste game! Without your sense of smell, that slice of pizza would be about as exciting as cardboard. So the next time you're savoring your favorite snack, remember to thank your nose for making it extra delicious!

Ever wonder why some people love broccoli while others think it tastes like punishment? It turns out, your genes might be playing a sneaky game of 'taste bud roulette!' Some folks are born with a genetic variation that makes certain vegetables taste incredibly bitter. So if your little one is adamant that Brussels sprouts are evil, they might not be trying to avoid eating their greens – their taste buds could be throwing a full-blown veggie revolt!

Here's a mind-bending fact: the color of your food can trick your brain into thinking it tastes different! That's right, your eyes are secret flavor influencers. For instance, an orange-colored drink might taste 'more orange-y' than a clear one, even if they're exactly the same flavor. So the next time you're trying to get your picky eater to try something new, you might want to consider giving their meal a colorful makeover. Who knows? That green ketchup might just be the key to veggie victory!

CHAPTER 9

CONCLUSION: KEEP LEARNING, KEEP LAUGHING

The Importance of Curiosity

Curiosity is the spark that ignites the fire of learning, and it's a flame we should never let die out! As families, we have the incredible opportunity to fan this flame together, turning everyday moments into exciting adventures of discovery. Whether it's wondering why the sky is blue or questioning why cats always land on their feet, embracing curiosity can lead us down fascinating paths of knowledge and laughter.

In our fast-paced world, it's easy to forget the joy of asking 'Why?' But remember, some of the greatest inventions and discoveries in history started with a simple, curious question. By encouraging curiosity in our children (and ourselves!), we're not just learning facts – we're developing problem-solving skills, fostering creativity, and building stronger family bonds. Plus, let's face it, the journey of finding out why flamingos are pink or how many licks it really takes to get to the center of a Tootsie Pop is just plain fun!

So, as we dive into this treasure trove of trivia, let's make a pact to keep our curiosity alive and kicking. Ask questions, seek answers, and don't be afraid to laugh at the wonderfully weird facts we'll uncover. After all, life is full of surprises, and with a curious mind, every day can be an exciting new episode of 'Did You Know?'. Get ready to amaze your friends, stump your parents, and giggle your way through a world of fascinating facts!

How to Find More Fun Facts

Now that you've journeyed through this fun-filled fact book, you might be wondering, 'Where can I find more amazing tidbits to share with my family?' Well, fear not, fact enthusiasts! The world is brimming with fascinating information just waiting to be discovered. From libraries bursting with quirky trivia books to educational websites that update daily with new facts, the possibilities are endless. Remember, every day is an opportunity to learn something new and tickle your funny bone!

One of the best ways to uncover more fun facts is to turn your everyday experiences into learning adventures. Visit museums, zoos, and science centers, where each exhibit is a goldmine of interesting information. Don't forget to read the plaques – they're often filled with surprising details that'll make you say, 'Did you know?' And here's a silly tip: try reading the back of cereal boxes or shampoo bottles. You never know what random facts you might find hiding in your own home!

Lastly, don't underestimate the power of asking questions and staying curious. Encourage your family to wonder about the world around them. Why do cats purr? How do airplanes stay in the sky? What makes popcorn pop? These questions can lead to delightful discoveries and hilarious discussions. Remember, the funniest facts often come from the most unexpected places. So keep your eyes peeled, your ears open, and your funny bone ready – you never know when the next amazing 'Did you know?' moment will strike!

Creating Your Own Family Fact Book

Now that you've explored the fascinating world of facts in this book, why not create your own family fact book? It's a fantastic way to bond with your loved ones while learning even more interesting tidbits about the world around you. Gather your family members and brainstorm topics that interest everyone - from your family's history to weird science facts you've discovered on your own. Remember, the sillier and more surprising the facts, the more fun you'll have!

To start your family fact book, choose a format that works for everyone. You could use a physical notebook, create a digital document, or even start a family blog. Assign different topics to family members and challenge them to find the most jaw-dropping facts they can. Don't forget to include funny anecdotes or personal experiences related to the facts - these will make your book uniquely yours and provide plenty of laughs during family gatherings.

As you build your family fact book, make it a regular activity to share and discuss new additions. You could have a weekly 'Fact Night' where everyone presents their latest discoveries. Not only will this keep the learning going, but it'll also create lasting memories and inside jokes that your family will cherish for years to come. Who knows? Your family fact book might even become a treasured heirloom, passed down through generations of curious minds!

How to Seduce Someone

So how exactly do you seduce someone? Beneath, a little series of steps offer a window into what is preferred to tempt somebody, how to make it happen, and how to deal with negative reactions. To seduce someone, you:

1. Start Touch:-
    The most important phase in luring somebody is starting contact. A long way from all out squeezing yourself into somebody's body, or quickly throwing yourself into a profound kiss, this touch is intended to make interest, intensity, and fascination, without serious actual contact. You can nonchalantly "knock" into somebody, with an apparently abashed, "Please accept my apologies," prior to moving along, or you can brush your leg against the object of your love's leg as you are plunking down. Indeed, even something as basic as raking your fingers over somebody's arm can have a strong and enduring effect.

2. Keep Down After Initiating:-
    In spite of the fact that you want to start some type of actual reach, you would rather not

support that contact for a really long time. After you "knock" into somebody, make some space between your bodies, while keeping eye to eye connection or visual interest alive. The intensity of introductory fascination can be additionally energized by interest and enthusiastic assumption.

3. Show Vulnerability:-
    Showing your weakness was viewed as a significant quality in certain examinations. At the point when men or ladies uncovered themselves as being nearly prey-like in their discourse, conduct, or position, the other gender was bound to show sexual interest. All types of people carried their hands to their necks and shoulders while attempting to convey a feeling of weakness, as the neck is perhaps of the most vulnerable put on the body, and setting your hand along your jaw, neck, or collarbone draws the object of your friendship's eyes there.

4. Occupy Room:-
    Acting tentative is definitely not a compelling method for enticing somebody while acting hesitant may be. One review exhibited that individuals who utilized more non-verbal

communication and moved in additional broad ways were bound to catch the interest of the individual they were keen on dating when contrasted and individuals who stood by or showed more shy ways of behaving while imparting. Putting yourself out there is fundamental to alluring somebody.

5. Cause Them To feel As Though Only They Matter:-
   At the point when you are attempting to tempt somebody, this isn't an ideal opportunity to explore every available opportunity. All things considered, ensure the individual you are keen on realizes that you are intrigued. Focus just to them- and even more alluring on the off chance that you can effectively brush another person off for them and let them in on how drawn in, awed, and energized you are by them. Giggle at their jokes, express interest in their accounts, and keep your eyes prepared for theirs. Scarcely any things more alluring than are being caused to feel that you are the main individual on the planet.

6. Make it happen
   Balance your temptation by spreading the word. To return home with somebody, say as much. If you have any desire to see them once more, you

can say that, as well. In the event that you are enticing your drawn-out accomplice, you should urge them to participate in another technique for foreplay with you, to switch things around. No matter what your definite objective or point, you complete your enticing method by demonstrating exactly what you need and pursuing it.

When to Back Down

On the off chance that somebody is radiating a sign of uneasiness or disappointment, it could be an ideal opportunity to quiet down and re-evaluate your technique. Certain individuals are not happy with individuals who are very forward with what they need, while others may be baffled by another person attempting to assume control in a new or existing relationship. Anything that the dynamic could be, your objective in tempting somebody ought not to be to unsettle, control, or force. All things considered, your objective in enticing is to let your forthcoming (or current) accomplice know the precisely exact thing you need, and precisely how you will get it.

On the off chance that somebody straightforwardly communicates their uneasiness that is an opportunity to withdraw. A renewed individual could let you know that you are coming on serious areas of strength excessively, and your accomplice could express something with the impact of, "I don't know I feel OK with this." While you could feel humiliated, you don't need to: you can make sense of what your point was, and have a discussion from that point. In the event that you end up reliably venturing over limits, or struggling with recognizing meaningful gestures, seeing a specialist could assist you with recapturing a few certainty and strength prior to deciding to tempt somebody.

Ways to be seductive

1. Being a tease joined by a quick street to an actual relationship:-
   Enchantment commonly engages in sexual relations as the essential ultimate objective although giving clues at the fascination, causing it to appear like you are drawn in, or through and through pronouncing your expectation could appear to be terrifying or overpowering, the craft of enticement is certainly not a surprising or disturbing errand. Done cautiously, and with a few understanding into the idea examples and ways of behaving of others, tempting somebody can make expanded identity regard and can assist you with broadening your relationship skylines.

2. There are a few circumstances where tempting somebody isn't the response:-
   These incorporate any circumstance where you or your ideal interest group feels dangerous, any circumstance including unfortunate or risky practices, or a circumstance including somebody who is busy. While it very well might be baffling to find that somebody you really like or have an interest in is hitched or in a relationship, this disclosure in no way, shape or form gives you the right or opportunity to attempt to split individuals up.
3. Luring somebody is something beyond being a tease, as it includes a more noteworthy measure of commitment and charm:-
   You can undoubtedly play with anybody you come into contact with, given the ideal opportunity, data, and level of solace. Tempting somebody, then again, is generally profoundly designated at the top of the priority list, while dating could have various final stages as a primary concern.
4. Enticing somebody includes causing them to feel like they are the main individual on the planet:-
   Building profound and actual closeness and power

through delicate, easygoing touch, prior to moving ceaselessly and making a practically actual requirement for closeness is the most ideal way to start the speciality of enchantment. A long way from being completely centred around thigh-high unmentionables, or obviously actual signals and ways of behaving, the craft of temptation generally includes the capacity to cause others to feel like they have the entirety of your consideration and all of your advantages which is the point at which you take the last action in putting your expectation, or expressing what you need. Now and again, you might be rebuked, however, the vast majority who have strolled through the means of enchantment will joyfully participate in anything you want assistance with.

The rules of seduction

1. Never control:

   Men and ladies hate to be controlled. It flags that either accomplice is effectively tricked. No relationship occurs in a vacuum, and each accomplice offers a set of experiences that would be useful. Subsequently, control can bring a profoundly charged feeling. Try not to make it happen.

2. Be free:

   Nobody prefers a poor individual. Men specifically prefer not to feel controlled or compelled. Assuming you are controlling, you can help him to remember his mom, and men would rather not be in a personal connection with their mother. Further, destitution conveys latent hostility. Accordingly, it is significant while meeting somebody and dating him interestingly to step back and see him as your own middle - - your own asset. Try not to stand by the telephone. Track down leisure activities and interests that you like. These will give you things to discuss, yet activities that are fascinating. On the off chance that you find some useful task to fulfil, you can share that life discussion. This main makes you really fascinating and energizing.

3. Act naturally:

   If you put on a show with the individual you are dating, you won't ever be aware assuming he really focuses on the genuine you. Moreover, commonality is vital to temptation, so he must have the option to depend on you to be you. To be personal requires transparency and close to home accessibility. Open individuals are without a doubt more helpless; in any case, fortune favours the bold. Try not to mess around and don't act shy; assuming that you mess around, your date will play with another person.

4. Switch off your telephone:

   Make an eye-to-eye connection and listen effectively. Men can't stand when a date is diverted and neither zeroed in on him nor at the time; it's limiting and annoying. Furthermore, when out on the town, don't check the room searching for or playing with others. It is simply inconsiderate. A significant piece of temptation is to esteem and approve the individual you are with, and on the off chance that you are not focusing, you will miss your second by giving some unacceptable impression.

5. Be unconstrained:
    Be fun-loving, be at the time and have a great time. This opens you to your true and fundamental self, which is the most appealing you will at any point be. The regular you, the un-layered you, give out that multitude of good undefended energies of fascination. Further, fun-loving nature flags a coy and prodding mentality that is non-forceful and says "come here."

6. Track down the humour:
    A fair of humour shows a decent character, and there isn't anything hotter in a man or a lady. Try not to think about things too severely or literally, don't be receptive; rather, be a decent game, and demonstrate the way that you can accept prodding as well as analysis.

7. Get individual:
    Find ways of being personal that have exceptional significance for simply you two. For instance: compose letters, and notes, and send amusing cards. It adds to expectation, tomfoolery and secret.

8. Unwind:
   Stress decrease means quite a bit to enchantment. Besides the fact that you be should loose, yet you need to have an inviting demeanour that assists your join forces with unwinding. On the off chance that you have issues around here, figure out how to contemplate, do moderate unwinding works out, go for strolls, pay attention to music and above all, get sufficient rest. Kids are grouchy when they don't get sufficient rest, as are grown-ups. A very much refreshed, tranquil individual can adapt to a wide range of tough spots.

9. Be a decent audience and show interest in your date:
   Ask about his biography before you spill every one of the beans about yours. Individuals love discussing themselves and love letting you know what their identity is. In the event that you are a decent audience, you will hear everything. Keep in mind: trust depends on experience. So when it's your chance to talk, it is smarter to quantify what you share, so then, at that point, you won't feel hurt or double-crossed on the off chance that your date isn't deserving of your trust.

10. Great Hygiene:

Pay regard to your appearance, your breath and your body cleanliness. Regardless of how charming you are, in the event that your cleanliness is hostile, you won't ever get a subsequent date. Furthermore, paying little mind to what you have heard, in the event that you don't invest wholeheartedly in your appearance, you might be managing weakness or low confidence.

11. Non-verbal communication:

Your non-verbal communication demonstrates regardless of whether you are sure. Be sure, smile and have an inspiring standpoint. Try not to exaggerate being a tease. Assuming you play with everybody, nobody will feel exceptional, esteemed or important.

At last, there is a scarcely discernible difference between tolerance and diligence. Allow your date an opportunity to be responsive - - never tense or rush the person. Temptation is a figment of your imagination, so the way that you introduce yourself is the means by which others will see you.

REFERENCES

https://www.regain.us/

https://fourminutebooks.com/

https://www.regain.us/

https://www.huffpost.com/

https://www.businessinsider.in/

Robert Greene